POSTCARD HISTORY SERIES

Yosemite's Historic Hotels and Camps

This vintage map postcard of Yosemite Valley shows the roads to many of the park's points of scenic interest. The more detailed map of Yosemite Village identifies several of the historic accommodations discussed in the book. These types of map postcards became popular in the 1950s, and there are several published of Yosemite. (Courtesy of Ron Chapman.)

ON THE FRONT COVER: The Sentinel Hotel was built in 1876 and was the first stop for stagecoaches arriving in Yosemite Valley. A popular hotel in the early 1900s, it provided magnificent views of Yosemite Falls and Half Dome. (Courtesy of Ron Chapman.)

ON THE BACK COVER: The Washburn family established Camp Yosemite in 1901 near Yosemite Falls. The camp, renamed Camp Lost Arrow in 1907, was able to accommodate up to 250 guests. It closed when Yosemite Lodge was completed in 1915. (Courtesy of the author.)

POSTCARD HISTORY SERIES

Yosemite's Historic Hotels and Camps

Alice van Ommeren

ARCADIA
PUBLISHING

Published by Arcadia Publishing
Charleston, South Carolina

Printed in the United States of America

Library of Congress Control Number: 2012954784

For all general information contact Arcadia Publishing at:
Telephone 843-853-2070
Fax 843-853-0044
E-mail sales@arcadiapublishing.com
For customer service and orders:
Toll-Free 1-888-313-2665

Visit us on the Internet at www.arcadiapublishing.com

CONTENTS

ACKNOWLEDGMENTS

The publications by Shirley Sargent were some of the most valuable resources in conducting the research for this book. It was a privilege to be able to review her work again in detail. Her reputation as a prolific writer and respected researcher on Yosemite history remains true. Another valuable resource was Lynne Greene's comprehensive inventory of Yosemite and its resources published in 1987 by the National Park Service. The dates, names, and places in the captions of this postcard book have been thoroughly researched to ensure accuracy, but some errors may be possible.

The postcards in this book are from my personal collection with a few exceptions. A special thanks goes to several other Yosemite postcard collectors who have shared vintage postcards from their collection to be included in this book. The postcard contributors are Ron Chapman, Jerry Kell, and Allen Elliott. The California History Room at the California State Library also donated some postcard images from its collection. Their contributions have been acknowledged in the captions, all other images appear courtesy of the author's postcard collection.

My gratitude goes out to several supporters of this project, including Rick Deutsch, Carol Jensen, and Ron Chapman. I also would like to acknowledge Marcy Protteau, who patiently and carefully edited the manuscript and provided valuable input. This book project could certainly not have been possible without the support of Frances Hutchins.

INTRODUCTION

Yosemite National Park, located on the western side of the Sierra Nevada Mountains, is a place of amazing natural splendor. A valley surrounded by polished granite domes and walls showcases several of the world's highest waterfalls. Yosemite is the keeper of such national treasures as Half Dome, Yosemite Falls, El Capitan, and Bridalveil Fall and is home to the beautiful Glacier Point, Wawona, and Tuolumne Meadows. Yosemite Valley and the surrounding areas were already inhabited by Native Americans when miners and explorers of European descent began finding their way there in 1851. It was only a few years later that the first tourists arrived. From the 1850s to the early 1900s, early pioneers and settlers faced incredible hardships and unbelievable challenges to build roads and accommodations that enabled others to experience this remarkable natural wonderland. After 1900, this struggle continued, but evolved towards a balance between building or renovating accommodations to increase visitation and protecting or preserving Yosemite's natural landscape. The steady flow of tourists and visitors and their changing needs for lodging and services has been central to Yosemite's overall development and history.

Privately printed postcards were first introduced in 1898, when Congress passed the Private Mailing Card Act. The act lowered the postal rates on private cards, resulting in increased demand for them. Until 1907, the backs of postcards were only allowed to contain the recipient's address, leaving the front for the image and the message. It was 1907 when postcards with a divided back were finally permitted. This meant the address and message shared space on the back and the image on the postcard could now take up the entire front. This change increased the popularity of postcards, launching an era referred to by collectors as the "Golden Age of Postcards."

During this period, the majority of postcards were printed in Germany, where lithography was considered an art and the printing presses were significantly more advanced than the ones in the United States. With the advent of World War I, imports from Germany declined and the nation's interest in postcards began to diminish. Cards continued to be published, but their quality waned and demand for them decreased.

Around 1930, "linen" postcards began to be printed on textured paper with a linen-like surface. In 1939, the photochrome postcard, or "chrome," was introduced and is still used today. These cards have glossy finishes and are easily produced using color photography. Real-photo postcards, also known as mailable photographs, were used as early as 1900. These cards, produced in small quantities by publishers or individuals, were difficult and expensive to produce and were generally less common, but this was not the case for Yosemite real-photo postcards. The park's natural beauty attracted significant photographic interest, and several photographers opened studios in the valley. They used the popularity of postcards in the early 1900s to their advantage by publishing and selling postcards of their photographs. Some of Yosemite's finest postcards were produced by such early and renowned photographers as J.T. Boysen, Arthur C. Pillsbury, and D.J. Foley.

The early 1900s were a significant period of development for lodging and accommodations in Yosemite, largely due to the establishment of the National Park Service as park administrators in 1916. The National Park Service delegated the management of services to a concessionaire whose function included improving existing accommodations to increase visitation. Upgrading the roads into the valley was also an important element of the park's plan. The construction of a year-round highway into the park and the building of weatherized lodging spurred the need to create activities that attracted tourists in the winter. This period of change coincided with the immense popularity of postcards, and therefore many aspects of this development have been documented for posterity in vintage postcards. Postcard collectors believe that the millions of postcards mailed from Yosemite to places across the world made the park world famous. It seemed that every park visitor felt compelled to send a postcard home.

The collection of postcards in this book chronicles Yosemite's accommodations from the early 1900s to the 1950s. This book does not give the complete history of Yosemite's hotels and camps, since not all accommodations were reflected on postcards. There are few postcards from before 1900, so images of many of the very early guesthouses were not captured. Most postcards were created to promote Yosemite as a tourist destination and, therefore, often only the most attractive establishments were featured. For example, there are very few postcards of the many campgrounds scattered around the valley, but there are many of the Ahwahnee Hotel. The book nevertheless provides a comprehensive illustration of how vintage postcards document an important period in the history of Yosemite. This collection of vintage postcards provides visitors with a better understanding and appreciation for the pioneer innkeepers and park concessionaires that laid the foundation for the hotels, lodges, camps, and sites available to us today in Yosemite National Park.

One

TRAVELING TO YOSEMITE

This 1906 postcard of a stagecoach approaching the Arch Rock entrance provides a glimpse of transportation to Yosemite before motorized vehicles. In those days, visiting Yosemite required a two-day trip from San Francisco to a town near Yosemite, followed by a challenging stagecoach or horseback journey across rocky roads weaving along steep mountainsides.

The Big Oak Flat Road, completed in 1874, became the second wagon road into Yosemite Valley from the north. It provided access for horse-and-wagon traffic before motor vehicles arrived in the early 1900s. After a rock slide and the completion of a shorter road, the Big Oak Flat Road was abandoned in 1945. This 1909 postcard provides a classic image of the historic road with its sharp, dusty switchbacks.

The other Yosemite Valley roads built in the 1870s were the Coulterville Road and the Wawona Road in the south. These roads provided access not only for horses but also for horse-drawn vehicles, which were the primary mode of transportation before the 1870s. The driver in this 1915 postcard holds the reins of his four-horse team as the stage travels into the valley along a dusty and narrow path.

The stagecoach era in Yosemite peaked in 1900 with several companies operating and competing for efficiency. Stations, like the one in this image, were spread along routes into the valley for exchanging horse teams and getting meals.

As more people traveled to Yosemite, the competition among the camps also increased, and improving accommodations and services became important. Camp Curry had a reputation for meeting the needs of its guests. A stagecoach with tired travelers is welcomed at the Camp Curry platform in this 1915 postcard.

The Yosemite Valley Railroad operated a line between Merced and Yosemite National Park from 1907 to 1945, carrying both freight and passengers. This is the station in Merced that serviced both the Santa Fe and Southern Pacific Railroad lines from Los Angeles and San Francisco. A fire burned down the station in 1929, but a duplicate was built on the same site. (Courtesy of Allen Elliott.)

2033 – Merced Canyon, California
on Line Yosemite Valley R. R.

The Yosemite Valley Railroad line follows the Merced River along the Merced Canyon for much of the way to El Portal. The lumber industry took advantage of the railroad as a source of transportation to supply the increasing demand for wood in California during the 1920s. Small towns developed along the railroad route in the following decades.

Beautiful California.
Merced Canon. Observatory Car, Yosemite Valley, R. R.
(On the road of a thousand wonders.)

The Yosemite Valley Railroad line, or "Short Line to Paradise," was completed at El Portal in May 1907. The train from Merced to the valley took approximately four hours. "The Road of a Thousand Wonders" was an advertising slogan of the Southern Pacific Company, whose rail lines extended from San Francisco to Los Angeles, and east to El Paso, New Orleans, Reno, and Ogden, as well as north to Portland.

The short railroad line ended at the park boundary in El Portal, where passengers would overnight at Del Portal Hotel. The next morning, visitors took the stage for a three-hour ride into the valley. The motor coach was introduced in 1913 and made that last part of the journey a lot faster. (Courtesy of Allen Elliott.)

El Portal Station, constructed in 1909, was the end of the line for the Yosemite Valley Railroad. This building replaced the smaller, more rustic station that serviced the first train to arrive from Merced at El Portal on May 15, 1907.

Del Portal Hotel was built in 1908 by the Yosemite Valley Railroad Terminal Company and provided overnight accommodations for Yosemite travelers who arrived at El Portal on the evening train. The four-story luxury hotel with a large lobby and two dining rooms, located just up the hill from the station, provided a comfortable stay for those continuing to the valley the next day.

A wide, covered veranda extended the length of Del Portal Hotel's ground floor. A ramp allowing tourists to board the stagecoaches for the trip to Yosemite Valley extended from the porch at the end of the hotel. Del Portal burned to the ground on October 27, 1917. In 1918, a less-extravagant structure known as El Portal Inn was constructed to replace the hotel.

This real-photo postcard is of the Tioga Pass Entrance Station, which was completed in 1910 at the summit of the Tioga Pass Road. Even though the first motorized vehicle entered Yosemite Valley in 1900, motor vehicles were banned from the park from 1907 to 1914 because of the dangerous roads. In other words, this image is from after 1914. (Courtesy of the California State Library.)

The wooden kiosk structure, developed with a rustic design, was completed in 1940. The kiosk served as the entrance station for several decades before being replaced. The printing on the back of this postcard says, "The Tioga Pass Entrance is at 9,941 feet high on the crest of the Sierra Nevada, which John Muir called, 'The Range of Light.' This, the east entrance, affords sparkling views of the 'high country.'"

The Tioga Pass Ranger Station is on the north side of the Tioga Road at the summit and was constructed in 1931, when much of the Tioga Pass Road was rebuilt. The one-bedroom residence and ranger station was the first stone building designed by the National Park Service in Tuolumne Meadows in the rustic architectural style. The color and texture of the building match the surrounding granite scenery.

The granite pillars that identify the entrance gates on each side of the Tioga Pass Road were built in 1934. The trip from the Tioga Pass Entrance Gate to Lee Vining in Mono County is 15 miles, through spectacular and scenic Lee Vining Canyon. Tioga Pass is the highest highway pass in California at 9,941 feet above sea level.

This postcard of the South Gate Entrance says, "The road to Yosemite from the south passes through dense forests of Sugar Pine, and mountain scenery of unusual beauty. As you enter the South gate entrance, the main road continues straight to Yosemite Valley, but a branch road leads to the famous Mariposa Grove of Big Trees, where may be seen the world's oldest living things."

The dustiness and steepness of the old Wawona Road led to the construction of the Wawona Tunnel as part of the park's renovations. The decision to bore through nearly a mile of solid granite was to achieve a better grade for the road and isolate the excavation. The blasting of the longest tunnel in the West at the time was completed in April 1933, after 29 months of drilling.

Inspiration Point provides travelers with their first glimpse of the valley as they emerge from the Wawona Tunnel. This is considered one of the most spectacular panoramic views of the valley and is one of the most popular sites in the park. The excavated materials from the Wawona Tunnel were used to construct this parking lot.

This 1950s postcard says, "Portal of Grandeur is a fitting name given that the east portal of the 4,233 foot Wawona road tunnel. Here may be seen the most comprehensive, sublime and beautiful view of Yosemite Valley, with El Capitan towering 3,600 feet at the left, Half Dome rising a mile high in the distance and the Three Graces with the ever changing beautiful Bridal Veil Fall on the right."

The Big Oak Flat Road Tunnel and Old Priest Grade lie between Moccasin and Big Oak Flat. The road is named for William Priest, who was a miner, an engineer, and one of the first Yosemite commissioners. The winding and steep road was first built in the 1850s as a wagon route called the Grizzly Gulch Road.

Two

WAWONA AND THE MARIPOSA GROVE

Pioneer Galen Clark settled the Wawona area, located four miles from Yosemite's south entrance, in 1857. Galen Clark was forced to sell his land in 1874 to the Washburn family, who subsequently built the Wawona Hotel, seven Victorian-style buildings constructed over several decades. This 1920s postcard shows early automobiles around the driveway of the main building of the Wawona Hotel, which opened in 1879.

Three of the Wawona Hotel buildings are captured in this 1950s postcard. In the right forefront is Little White, a building completed in 1884 and designed to serve as the hotel manager's residence. Next to Little White is Clark's Cottage, or Long White, the oldest structure in the complex. It was built in 1876, just a few years prior to the main building seen in the background.

The building on the right in this postcard is the annex. It was built in 1917, around the same time as the swimming pool and golf course were completed, and was one of the last buildings of the Wawona Hotel complex to be constructed. This large wooden-frame structure is surrounded by a two-story veranda and has 39 guest rooms, 20 of which have private baths.

The predominant structure in this postcard is the main building, which was built in 1879 on the actual site of Galen Clark's original settlement. Clark's Cottage, on the far right, was built in 1876. It was the only building to survive the 1878 fire that destroyed most of the buildings at this site, which was then called Clark's Station. The Washburn family rebuilt the complex as the Wawona Hotel.

The Wawona Golf Course, opened in 1918, was the first regulation golf course in the Sierra Nevada and the first within the boundary of a national park. The nine-hole golf course was designed and built by Walter Favarque. Wawona Golf Course is one of the few organic golf courses in the country, where no pesticides are applied and only reclaimed water is used for irrigation.

This is a very early postcard, taken in 1900, of the Wawona Hotel's main building. One of the unique features of the Wawona Hotel is its location on the edge of a hill overlooking the meadow. The Wawona Hotel was declared a National Historical Landmark in 1987 and is the largest remaining Victorian hotel complex in a national park. (Courtesy of Allen Elliott.)

The circular driveway that leads up to the main building is lined with cobblestones that came from the nearby river. The stone fountain in the center of the driveway in front of the hotel dates back to the hotel's opening and was recently renovated. The main building's lobby, dining room, lounge, and sitting room date from the 1910s, when the building's interior was extensively remodeled.

Galen Clark originally constructed the Wawona Covered Bridge in 1857 as an open-deck bridge. It spans the South Fork of the Merced River on one of the original stage roads from Wawona to Yosemite Valley. The bridge was covered after the Washburns bought it in 1875. The bridge is one of 12 remaining covered bridges in California.

Galen Clark discovered a grove of giant Sequoias known today as the Mariposa Grove of the Big Trees. In order to make it accessible to tourists, he built a trail from Wawona to the grove. He also built a cabin in the grove in the 1860s that served as an office and visitors' stop. This postcard shows the cabin after it was rebuilt by the State of California in 1885.

The cabin was enlarged in 1902 to accommodate a gift shop. The structure became known as the "Galen Clark Cabin" and was used in many early postcards to emphasize the scale of the giant trees in the grove. This cabin was replaced in 1930 by a new structure that resembles the original and, to this day, serves as the Mariposa Grove Museum.

Yosemite has three groves of giant Sequoia trees; the largest grove is the Mariposa Grove of the Big Trees. The Mariposa Grove is located near Yosemite's south entrance and was one of the earliest big-tree groves to attract public interest. The Grizzly Giant captured on this postcard is one of the largest and oldest living Sequoia trees and is estimated to be 2,700 years old.

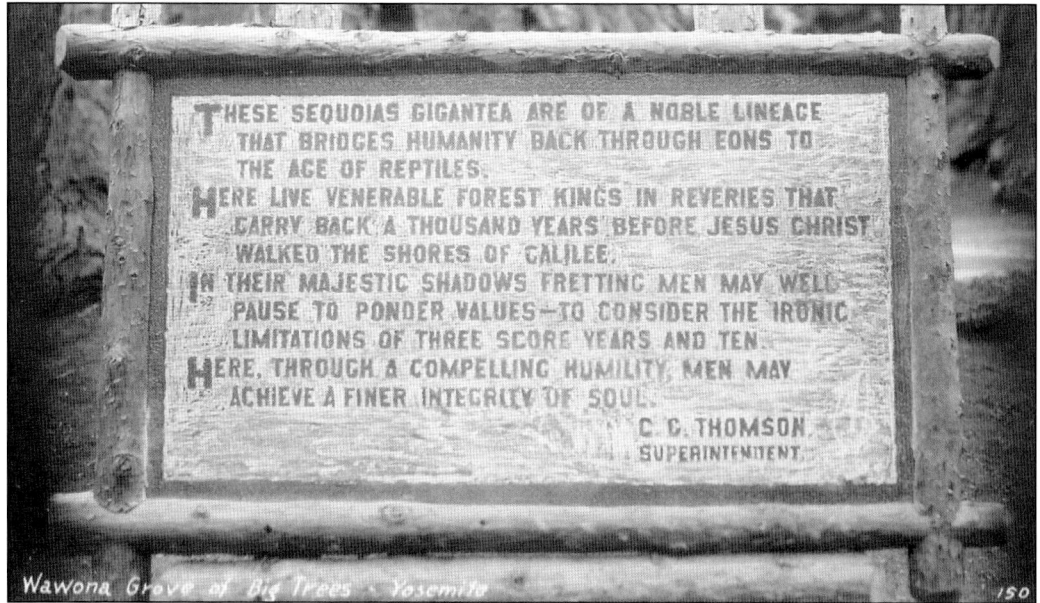

Charles Goff Thomson was the superintendent of Yosemite National Park from 1927 until his death in 1937. In 1930, he initiated a comprehensive sign program with the intent of providing information to visitors. Special redwood signs with burned lettering were placed throughout the Mariposa Grove of the Big Trees. This one is inscribed with Thomson's poetic perception of the grove.

15172—WAWONA, BIG TREE,
YOSEMITE VALLEY, CALIFORNIA
4,846 YEARS OLD AND REACHING
TO A HEIGHT OF 372 FEET.

The tunnel cut through the Wawona Tree in 1881 made it the most famous tree in the Mariposa Grove and a popular tourist attraction for almost a century. Many postcards were published of horse-drawn carriages and motor vehicles driving through or stopped under the tree. The Wawona Tree fell during record snow in 1969 and is now referred to as the Fallen Wawona Tunnel Tree.

Big Trees Yosemite Valley, Cal.

At one time, there were two tunnel trees in the Mariposa Grove, the Wawona Tunnel Tree and the California Tunnel Tree. The California Tunnel Tree, carved out in 1895, provided road access for the horse-drawn stages. Preservation and protection movements in the 1930s and the relocation of the main road ended the practice of driving through the tree. The California Tunnel Tree remains a tourist attraction today.

One of the most frequently photographed fallen Sequoias is the Fallen Monarch, which is still located near the entrance of the grove. It is generally thought that this tree fell down several centuries ago and has been preserved by the tannic acid in the wood, which stops the tree's decay. There are many vintage postcards of the Fallen Monarch with various people shown in various positions and predicaments.

A souvenir postcard from the 1910s shows 36 US Cavalry men and their horses on top of and alongside the Fallen Monarch. The Cavalry kept law and order in Yosemite National Park from its founding in 1890 until 1916, when the National Park Service was created. The cavalry often posed with the Fallen Monarch for Southern Pacific Railroad publicity photographs and postcards.

This open pavilion structured around the Montana Tree served as the office of a wooden cabin and tent complex established in the Mariposa Grove in the 1920s. The back of this 1925 postcard reads, "Grandmother is sitting in this little rustic terrace writing you a line. Little trees out here grow to be big trees—just as little girls grow up to be big girls."

The Big Trees Lodge was built in 1932 near Sunset Point in the center of the Mariposa Grove, replacing the earlier camp of wooden cabins and tents established in the 1920s in the upper portion of the grove. Eldridge Spencer designed the lodge with 12 guest rooms, an office, a store, and a studio.

MARIPOSA GROVE BIG TREES LODGE

The small and attractive Big Trees Lodge at the Mariposa Grove had a reputation for providing restful accommodations and distinctive meals served on the outdoor terrace. This postcard of the outside dining patio was mailed in 1942.

In 1972, the Big Trees Lodge closed to tourists and instead became a dorm for Youth Conservation Corps groups. In 1982, fire and a fallen tree destroyed the roof of the Big Trees Lodge, leading to the lodge's eventual demolition. The site has slowly returned to its natural state.

Three

CAMP CURRY

David and Jennie Curry, who were committed to settling in Yosemite and providing visitors with affordable room and board, founded Camp Curry in 1899. The camp was established at the east end of Yosemite Valley at the base of Glacier Point and started as a dozen tents, eventually growing into the large complex of accommodations and services known today as Curry Village.

Camp Curry had almost 50 tents in its second season, including two large dining tents that were used for cooking and serving meals. The sleeping facilities were simple, but dining at a table with linens and dishes was important to guests. The Curry family put great significance in interacting with their guests, and this resulted in nightly hosted campfires, guided day hikes, and a choice of various outdoor activities.

The first permanent structure at Camp Curry was constructed in 1901 and served as a dining room and kitchen. This was followed by the building of a registration office, which still stands today but serves as a lounge instead, in 1904. The original dining building was destroyed by fire in 1912 but was rebuilt with the addition of a gift shop and cafeteria.

Large campfires for guests were an important ritual at Camp Curry. This postcard shows several park officials gathered around the campfire next to the Camp Curry Studio and Soda Fountain. Jennie Curry really liked this image and had it made into a postcard.

Foster Curry designed this entrance gate around 1914 for his parents, David and Jennie Curry, the founders of Camp Curry. The rustic gate is located near the current registration office and has been a welcome sign for Camp Curry for a century. Foster Curry followed in his father's footsteps by working at the Curry Company until it dissolved in 1973.

Forty-eight rustic-style cabins were built at Camp Curry between 1918 and 1922 in order to provide increasingly more-comfortable accommodations. The furnished duplex cabins provided guests with electricity, hot running water, and shared baths. In 1924, a series of one-room cabins without baths were added to the camp.

Camp Curry put great emphasis on providing guests with a pleasant dining experience. This postcard of Camp Curry's terrace dining was mailed from the Camp Curry post office on August 9, 1926. It states the following: "We arrived here Friday PM, found the roads better than expected, and enjoyed the trip very much. Drove to Big Trees from Wawona Friday AM, beautiful, beautiful."

Recreational activities were important to Camp Curry's success as a family accommodation. As early as 1902, tennis and croquet courts were laid out. These were followed by the construction of a swimming pool in 1913. By the 1920s, recreational opportunities at Camp Curry included nightly variety shows and music, a children's playground, a bowling alley, and a poolroom. (Courtesy of the California State Library.)

The swimming pool, built in 1913, was constructed of a unique assembly of mortared river cobbles used for both the tank and the adjoining bathhouse. The bathhouse included showers when first built, and in 1920, beauty and barbershops were added. Fire destroyed the bathhouse and pool in 1977. This was a devastating loss as they both had great historical value to Camp Curry.

The Soda Fountain at Camp Curry was built in 1921 in the Studio building, a central complex that included dining and shopping facilities. The Soda Fountain with its "spotless candy kitchen" was a popular venue after evening programs since it sold soda, candy, ice cream, and hot chocolate, as well as cigarettes.

This card, postmarked in 1945, says, "Howard and I had dinner in the dining room pictured. The food and service was quite a far cry from that at camp." This dining room at Camp Curry seated nearly 900 guests. It burned down in 1973 but was rebuilt with many of the original interior designs.

This 1926 postcard shows the fireplace in the Camp Curry Studio. Camp Curry was located on the cooler side of the valley, and so many of its buildings were designed with fireplaces, which were often made with river rock. The use of bear hides as rugs was common during that period.

This postcard shows Curio Corner at the Camp Curry Studio. The gift shop sold various paintings and photographs, as well as Native American baskets and weavings. In 1917, Camp Curry began producing and selling its own postcards as a way of promoting the accommodations. These vintage postcards of Camp Curry have been valuable in preserving its history.

The evening entertainment was an important element of the Camp Curry experience. In 1915, the south veranda of the registration building was converted into a stage for nightly readings and talks. This postcard shows Grace Roger Jilson, who was a popular storyteller at Camp Curry for several seasons in the late 1910s. This stage was replaced by the amphitheater in 1953.

The "Bird Man of Yosemite" was an early and popular tourist attraction. Herbert Sonn arrived in Yosemite in 1914 from New Jersey and was determined to stay. He was fascinated by animals and started creating and selling bird caricatures from natural materials, such as pinecones, acorns, stems, roots, and bark. This is a 1930s postcard of the Bird Man's Curry camp, located at the foot of the Ledge Trail.

First conceptualized by Mountain House builder James McCauley, the Yosemite Firefall was a ceremony during which burning coals were pushed over the top of Glacier Point, creating a glowing firefall. David Curry reestablished it in the early 1900s to become a popular summer ritual. David Curry himself called up to Glacier Point each evening to signal when the firefall could begin. The last Yosemite Firefall occurred on January 25, 1968.

CAMP CURRY'S FIRE FALL.

This postcard says, "The Fire on Glacier Point. At 9 p.m. on summer evenings the Firefall flares from the darkness of Glacier Point. At the conclusion of the nightly campfire entertainment, the burning embers are pushed from the ledge, 3,200 feet above the Valley and a cataract of fire falls nearly 900 feet in a glowing cascade of orange and red."

Camp Curry is much colder than other areas of Yosemite Valley because of its shady location at the foot of Glacier Point. The completion of the All-Year Highway in 1926 and the increasing popularity of winter sports certainly influenced Camp Curry to provide additional accommodations during the winter months. In 1929, visitors used the Curry bungalows for the first time.

In order to encourage tourism during the winter, an ice-skating rink was opened in 1929 on a large parking lot east of the Camp Curry complex. Portable buildings with a "northern European design" surrounded the rink and were used as warming huts. This card, postmarked on February 23, 1941, shows the entrance to the ice rink with snow-covered Half Dome as a backdrop.

This postcard is from a series of "winter activities" cards published in the 1930s to promote Yosemite as a year-round destination. This ice rink at the foot of Glacier Point has temporary bleachers and outdoor lighting. Before this ice rink was constructed in 1929, a "natural" ice rink was created each winter by spraying the parking lot in front of Camp Curry with water.

The park introduced many winter activities for Yosemite visitors in the late 1920s, where some succeeded and some failed. The ice rink at Camp Curry became one of the most successful. The ice rink was used for many types of programs and activities, including ice hockey. To this day, an ice-skating rink is still erected every winter; however, the original was much larger and more decorative than the modern one.

In 1927, a four-track toboggan run was constructed just west of Camp Curry at the old sawmill site, not far from the LeConte Memorial. The toboggan slide claimed to offer "mile-a-minute thrills in a setting of incomparable scenic beauty." It became a popular attraction but was removed in the 1950s after a series of accidents.

Four

GETTING AROUND THE VALLEY

Tourist parties on mules and horses were everyday scenes at the foot of the Yosemite Valley trails during the busy summers of the early 1900s. Mules were favored because they were more predictable and dependable on the trail. This card was postmarked December 6, 1909, and says, "Ready for the Trail," on the reverse side.

A postcard of a horse party traveling toward Nevada Fall has printing on the back saying, "Nevada Fall is the second fall in that beautiful spot, and the question as to which falls is the most beautiful, the Bridal Fall or the Nevada Fall, is much argued. This picture shows some tourists on a high bluff viewing the Falls."

The Zig Zag Trail is steep, winding, and stretches between Liberty Cap and Nevada Fall. At the top of the trail it splits, leading to Clouds Rest on the left and to Glacier Point on the right. Although challenging, trails like this one have made many areas in Yosemite more accessible to horseback and hiking parties.

This horse party is at one of the highest points on the trail, across from Liberty Cap with Nevada Fall in the background. Liberty Cap lies at the extreme northwestern margin of Little Yosemite Valley, adjacent to Nevada Fall. It rises 1,700 feet from the base of Nevada Fall to a peak elevation of 7,080 feet.

A wrangler leads horses and mules on the Horse Trail with Nevada Fall in the background. Lafayette Bunnell was a Yosemite explorer who suggested the name "Nevada" for the waterfall because it is the nearest waterfall to the Sierra Nevada. Horseback and mule rides on this trail are still available today.

These were among the first motor vehicles to carry tourists from El Portal into Yosemite, beginning in 1913. This 1920s advertising postcard "A Moreland in the Yosemite National Park" has the back printed with "Manufactured in Los Angeles in one of the largest Motor Truck factories in the United States . . . Six different sizes from 1,500 to 13,000 pounds capacity, if interested send for literature."

The automobile revolutionized travel and increased visitation to Yosemite in the late 1910s. As more visitors came into the park independently, the public and the private sector demanded fewer tolls and also wanted road improvements. This car poses with Bridalveil Fall, which drops 617 feet and flows year-round. It is the first waterfall many travelers see as they arrive in the valley. (Courtesy of Ron Chapman.)

Yosemite Valley has a series of bridges, most of which cross the Merced River. The bridges are known for their use of local granite and arched configurations. The last one built was Stoneman Bridge, which replaced a wooden bridge at the Camp Curry intersection. The Stoneman Bridge was completed in 1933 and has a unique single arch.

Famous for its view of Half Dome, Sentinel Bridge was the sixth bridge built over the Merced River and leads toward Yosemite Village from the south. The Sentinel Bridge version on this postcard was built in 1919, replacing an iron bridge from 1878, which had replaced a wooden bridge. The current bridge was built in 1993 with a wider arch to allow for the river's water to flow more slowly.

Winter activities were available in Yosemite as early as the 1910s, especially snowshoeing and ice-skating. The establishment of the Winter Club in 1928 and the park's commitment to more year-round attractions led to an increase in winter activities. For a short period in the 1930s, dog sledding was popular but was quickly discontinued due to the challenges of dog boarding and inconsistent snow coverage in the valley.

SLEIGH RIDING IN THE YOSEMITE VALLEY

Another popular wintertime activity in Yosemite Valley was sleigh riding; although, there was not always enough snow. This image is from a winter activity postcard series that was used as a publicity effort to entice people to make Yosemite their winter destination.

The Lost Arrow Trail opened in 1929 near the Yosemite Creek footbridge and Yosemite Falls and became one of the earliest efforts to build a nature trail in a national park. The Lost Arrow Trail passes by a plaque that identifies the location of John Muir's cabin, a few feet away from the memorial bench dedicated in 1911 to Galen Clark, the first Guardian of the Yosemite Grant.

Sightseeing of Half Dome or South Dome, as it was called at one time, has always been a popular Yosemite activity. The back of this postcard says, "This huge dome dominated the eastern end of the valley and has an elevation of 8,852 feet above sea level, rising 4,941 feet above the valley floor. The face of it is cut sheer and noticeably concave for approximately 2,000 feet."

The Royal Arches, the North Dome and Washington Column, from Camp Curry, Yosemite, California

The Royal Arches are located at the north end of the valley and are recognizable by the cliff's semicircular exfoliation of granite. This postcard was mailed in October 1908, almost two decades before the construction of the Ahwahnee Hotel in 1927. The Royal Arches have become a popular climbing area, spanning from Church Bowl to Washington's Column.

Tourists lost in Admiration over Nature's Wonders in "Beautiful Yosemite Valley, California."

This view of Yosemite Valley from Old Inspiration Point greeted the men of the Mariposa Battalion who first entered this valley on March 21, 1851. The Southern Pacific Railroad published this 1910s postcard for promotional purposes. "Yosemite Valley, California, On the Line of the S.P.R.R." is printed on the back of the card.

1510 — MIRROR LAKE IN WINTER, YOSEMITE

Mirror Lake and Mt. Watkins. Yosemite Valley, California

Mirror Lake was one of Yosemite's most popular attractions, which is evident from the variety of postcards made of the seasonal lake located at the entrance of Tenaya Canyon at the base of Half Dome. It is the last remnant of a large glacial lake that once filled most of Yosemite Valley and is vanishing slowly due to sediment accumulation.

Mirror Lake is named for the way its clear and motionless surface reflects the surrounding mountains, including Mount Watkins and Half Dome. In the 1860s, Capt. William James Howard built a summerhouse on the lake's shore, with a large dance floor extended out over the water. The Mirror Lake House was a favorite nightspot and could be reached by a one-mile road.

Happy Isles is a group of islands in the Merced River at the eastern end of Yosemite Valley. The site was first called Island Rapids by pioneer James Hutchings but was renamed Happy Isles by Yosemite Guardian W.E. Dennison; this was because "no one can visit them without for the while forgetting the grinding strife of his world and being happy." The scenic spot is the gateway to the valley's most popular hikes.

Stephen Mather was the first director of the National Park Service. His influence on the park service system led them to erect bronze plaques in every park with the words, "He laid the foundation of the National Park Service, defining and establishing the policies under which its areas shall be developed and conserved, unimpaired for future generations. There will never come an end to the good that he has done."

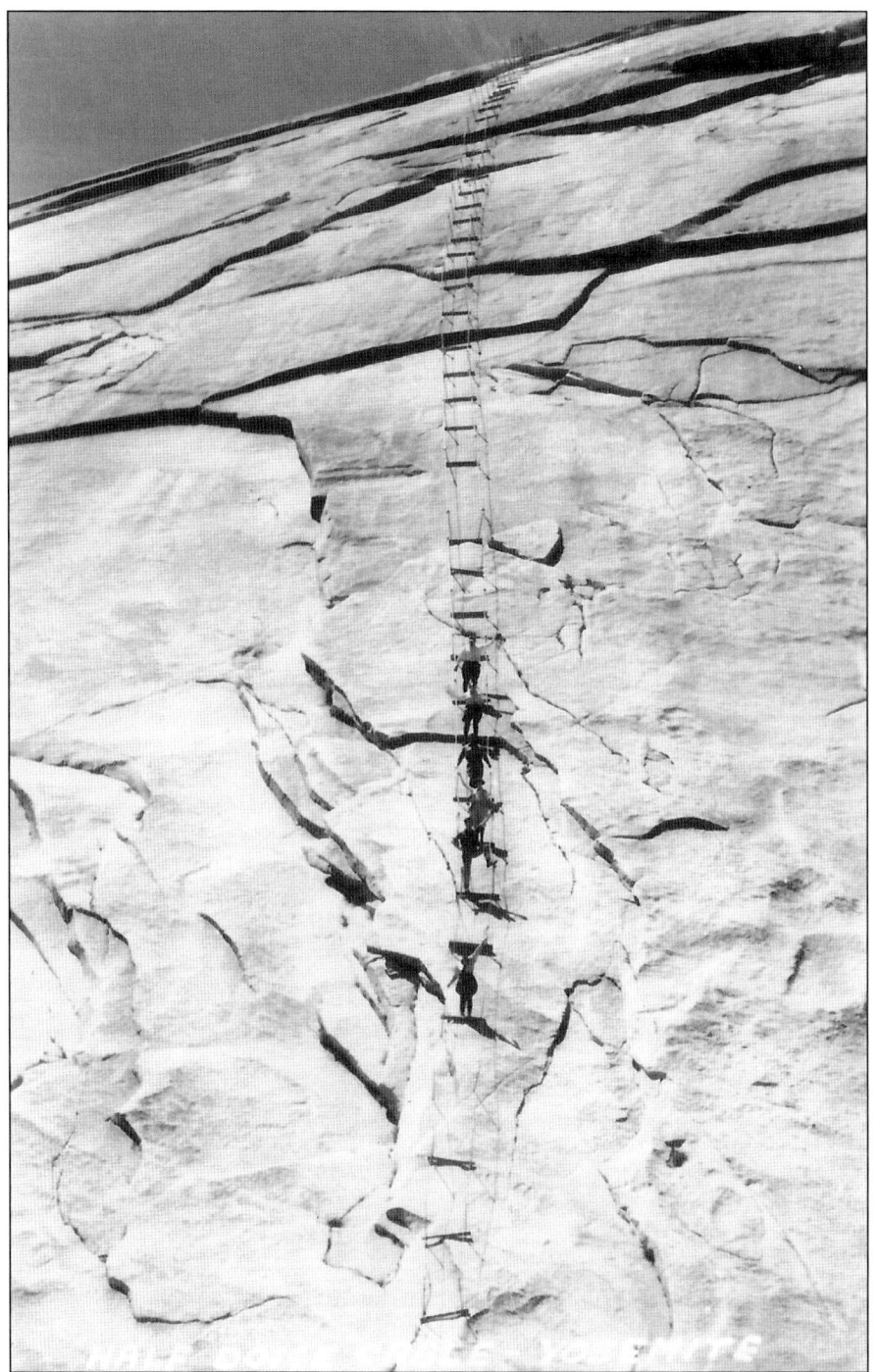

Yosemite's most popular rock formation is Half Dome, which rises almost 5,000 feet above the valley floor. Thousands of people a year make the challenging 16-mile round-trip hike to the summit. This 1940s postcard shows the most famous part of the hike, scaling up the cables. Two metal cables, first installed in 1919, allow hikers to climb the last 400 feet of steep staircase to the summit.

Five

OTHER CAMPS
IN YOSEMITE VALLEY

The success of Camp Curry and the increasing interest in Yosemite as a tourist destination in the early 1900s led to the establishment of other commercial camps in the park. Camp Ahwahnee was created in 1908 near the base of the famous Four-Mile Trail to Glacier Point. It became the first camp that stagecoaches reached when traveling from El Portal to Yosemite Valley.

Camp Ahwahnee was established in an open pine forest at the foot of Sentinel Rock, facing Yosemite Falls. This once was the location of the village of Loi'-ah, a large camp of Yosemite indigenous peoples. Camp Ahwahnee opened in May 1908 and was operated by William Sell for seven years before the Desmond Park Service Company bought the camp and subsequently closed it in 1917.

The establishment of Camp Ahwahnee generated immediate competition with Camp Curry. Although it was never as successful as Camp Curry, Camp Ahwahnee made great efforts to attract guests by promoting its more modern amenities, including bathrooms with hot and cold water and a large dining room with magnificent views. This postcard was mailed on June 30, 1911.

This postcard was mailed to San Francisco in July 1910 with "I am having a lovely visit in the Yosemite Valley at this delightful Camp" written on the back. The image provides a great view of a stagecoach entering Camp Ahwahnee with Yosemite Falls in the background.

The Camp Ahwahnee dining room was a large open-framed building with a splendid view of Yosemite Falls. This card of the dining room was mailed from El Portal on August 30, 1912, to Frank Webster at Camp Ahwahnee, stating the following: "My dear husband, we arrived at El Portal at twenty minutes past five. I suspect you are very lonely. I was very sorry to leave you, love from Catherine."

This postcard of the sitting room and office of Camp Ahwahnee was mailed from El Portal on June 12, 1913. There is sparse documentation on Camp Ahwahnee, but a nice series of early postcards provides images of many aspects of the camp.

Camp Yosemite was founded near Yosemite Falls in 1901, before Camp Ahwahnee, and was also a rival of Camp Curry. Camp Yosemite was owned by the Washburn family, owners of the Wawona Hotel, and operated by Jay Cook, who also ran the Sentinel Hotel.

Camp Yosemite was not as successful as Camp Curry but it certainly thrived because of its shady location near the falls and the camp's famous host, Yosemite pioneer Galen Clark. The camp was actually located in a grove of black oak trees on the former site of the Hutchings Sawmill, where John Muir worked until 1871.

In 1906, the government named its military post Camp Yosemite, and to avoid confusion, Camp Yosemite was renamed Camp Lost Arrow. Camp Lost Arrow had tents to accommodate up to 250 guests and had several office buildings, a dining room, a kitchen, bathhouses, and lavatories. The camp closed when construction of Yosemite Lodge began in 1915.

This postcard provides a rare view of the interior of the office at Camp Lost Arrow, formerly known as Camp Yosemite. The camp opened in 1901 near the foot of Lower Yosemite Fall and was renamed Camp Lost Arrow, after the spire or detached pillar adjacent to Upper Yosemite Fall, in 1907. The office provided a place of relaxation where vacationers could write postcards and letters.

In May 1915, the Desmond Park Service Company was contracted by the National Park Service to expand and manage Yosemite's accommodations. One of their first endeavors was the leasing of the former Army campsite near Yosemite Falls. They swiftly renovated the Army barracks into a tourist camp, which became known as Yosemite Falls Camp. This Desmond "Yosemite Falls" Camp postcard was mailed on August 17, 1915.

The back of this 1918 postcard says, "Yosemite Falls Camp—Enjoy one of the finest locations in the valley in close proximity to Yosemite Falls and a short distance from the village. The view is taken in front of the large dining room and the tents and wooden bungalows are hidden under the majestic pines and redwoods. The camp has a fine swimming pool, tennis court and other attractions."

YOSEMITE NTL. PARK-BEAR

The growth of tourism, and therefore camps, in the early 1900s led to an increase in the number of bears, specifically the American black bear, which fed on garbage left by visitors. Despite its name, most of these bears are not black but rather various shades of brown. The bears turned into a problem by the 1920s, as they became more assertive in accessing food supplies and searching through the garbage pits.

This postcard is labeled as "Chief Ranger Townsley, with his Pet Cub Bear." In the early 1920s, the National Park Service used the feeding of bears as a tourist attraction. Special platforms with lighting were created to feed the bears, drawing large crowds of spectators after dark. These bear shows were discontinued in 1940, and a large number of bears were relocated outside the valley at this time.

Various types of wildlife are represented on vintage postcards of Yosemite. This 1940s postcard shows a mule deer buck. Mule deer are found throughout the park and are unusually tame. They exhibit great curiosity, making them a favorite among park visitors. Their coloring makes them difficult to see in the brush, but the flapping of their big mule-like ears will often give them away.

This 1940s postcard of two fledgling California spotted owls is evidence that Yosemite was a bird-watcher's paradise. This subspecies of spotted owls resides in old-growth forests on the western slopes of the Sierra Nevada. Their populations have declined over the decades due to habitat loss and competition from other owls. The California spotted owls are federally listed as a threatened species but persist in certain areas of Yosemite.

This postcard is of the Government Camp near Yosemite Falls. Government Camps were built and numbered by the State of California in the late 1880s and free to visitors who brought camping equipment. Before these camps were established, there were no restrictions on camping in the valley, which meant campers could stake tents anywhere, and most campers did this either along the Merced River or in open meadows.

Camping remained popular after the development of hotels and commercial camps. In the early 1900s, five camps located west of Yosemite Village, Camp 1 through Camp 5, were abandoned for sanitary reasons. The development of public campgrounds east of the valley continued. In the 1970s, the campgrounds were finally given names to replace their numbers. This 1927 postcard shows one of the camps along the Merced River.

Six

GLACIER POINT HOTEL

The three-story Glacier Point Hotel was built in 1917 at more than 3,000 feet above the Yosemite Valley floor. Its location on the south rim afforded it one of the most spectacular views in the world. The structure to the right of the hotel is Mountain House, which was completed in 1873. In 1969, both buildings burned to the ground in one of Yosemite's worst fires.

The Glacier Point Hotel and Mountain House were closed during the winter season. Nevertheless, it snowed frequently, and the harsh weather took its toll on the wood-framed hotels over the decades. There were no guests during the winter season, but the caretakers often stayed to maintain the hotel and became isolated from the outside world by snow. (Courtesy of Allen Elliott.)

Yosemite pioneer James McCauley built Mountain House, the two-story hotel at Glacier Point, in 1873. Several years earlier, he had commissioned John Conway to build a four-mile toll road to Glacier Point from the base of Sentinel Rock in Yosemite Valley. This trail was the only feasible route to Glacier Point until 1882.

The wood used to build Mountain House in 1873 came from the surrounding forest. Other construction materials had to be carried by mules up the Four-Mile Trail. The sparse bathing facilities and inadequate interior partitions discouraged many tourists from staying overnight in Mountain House.

In 1882, the Yosemite Stage and Turnpike Company built a 14-mile wagon road across to Glacier Point from Chinquapin. This doubled business for the Glacier Point accommodations. Extensive repairs were made to Mountain House in 1895, but it never became suitable for tourists. After the Glacier Point Hotel was built in 1917, Mountain House served as housing for employees and a cafeteria for the public. (Courtesy of Allen Elliott.)

This postcard provides an unusual view of the entrance to the Glacier Point Hotel. A 1930 advertisement says, "At Glacier Point the motorist finds a modern hotel, offering lodging and meals at reasonable rate. Nearby is a Government Camp for those with their own camping equipment. An overnight stop affords an opportunity to enjoy the magnificent view in changing light and color effects."

Glacier Point was a popular tourist destination, but the hotel, for a variety of reasons, never reached its anticipated success. The hotel had a short season, which led to higher room rates, and most guests only stayed for one night. The Yosemite Valley itself was where most visitors wanted to spend extended periods of time.

The Glacier Point Hotel was built with 80 rooms and was able to accommodate approximately 180 guests. This postcard of the hotel lobby includes a glimpse of the fireplace, which is two-sided and shared with the dining room on the other side. Many people visited Glacier Point just for the day, which meant that the hotel gift shop and accompanying cafeteria were always busy.

The Glacier Point Hotel had a large fireplace where guests gathered in the evenings after dinner. This fireplace and chimney were the only structural pieces still standing after an accidental fire consumed the hotel on August 9, 1969.

Glacier Point provides an impressive view straight down into Yosemite Valley. This postcard is looking the half-mile down to Camp Curry, now referred to as Curry Village, which is located at the foot of Glacier Point. This was also the location of the nightly firefall, a summer event of pushing burning embers and coals from Glacier Point to create a fire waterfall for Curry guests.

This postcard of the porch or "tables at the cafeteria" gives a sense of the infinite panoramic vista that included an impressive view of Half Dome. There were no other accommodations in Yosemite that afforded such a spectacular outlook. Visitors would spend hours admiring the panoramic landscape.

The veranda, which stretched across the back of the Glacier Point Hotel, faced east toward Half Dome. Overnight guests of the hotel lingered on this porch, along with guests on daytrips to Glacier Point and overnighters from the campground located south of the complex.

Glacier Point provides one of the best views of Half Dome, including the rock formation's backside. The Half Dome summit was considered inaccessible until George Anderson conquered it in October 1875. He constructed a route on the dome's backside by drilling and placing iron eyebolts into the smooth granite. The 16-mile round trip from the valley floor to the top of Half Dome is a very popular hike today.

3012 - Yosemite Valley, California. - Pack Mules, Glacier Point

As early as 1864, tourist parties were guided to Glacier Point. This postcard of pack mules was mailed on December 28, 1909. The Four-Mile Trail, which is now actually closer to five miles long, leaves from Yosemite Valley near Swinging Bridge and climbs 3,200 feet to Glacier Point.

STARTING FOR GLACIER POINT YOSEMITE VALLEY, CALIFORNIA.

This postcard shows a large group of tourists on mules starting for Glacier Point. There are two trails to Glacier Point from Yosemite Valley—the Four-Mile Trail, which starts near Swinging Bridge at the base of Sentinel Rock, and the Panorama Trial, which starts near Vernal and Nevada Falls. The Panorama Trail is nearly twice as long as the Four-Mile Trail and provides a different perspective.

This early postcard shows Taft Point, named after Pres. William Howard Taft, who visited Yosemite in 1909. The trail from Glacier Point Road to the point is about a mile long and provides incredible views of the valley, including Yosemite Falls and El Capitan. Taft Point is also notable as the location of giant fissures, which are cracks in the granite that stretch down to the valley floor.

This Jeffrey pine on Sentinel Dome was one of the most photographed trees in the world and the subject of numerous postcards. The pine was photographed as early as 1867 by Carlton Watkins, but its most famous moment was in 1940, when it became the subject of a photograph by Ansel Adams. Although the tree died in the drought of 1976, it stayed on Sentinel Dome until 2003.

1438 – OVERHANGING ROCK, GLACIER POINT, YOSEMITE VALLEY, CALIFORNIA.

The famous Overhanging Rock is considered one of the earliest, as well as most frequently photographed, subjects of images of Glacier Point. This 1908 postcard by San Francisco publisher Edward H. Mitchell was copied by numerous postcard publishers over the decades. The 10-foot-wide ledge is photographed from a slightly lower level looking eastward with the extended rock and people profiled against the sky.

At 7,000 feet in elevation, Glacier Point provides an endless panoramic view of domes, peaks, ridges, ranges, and waterfalls. This 1920s postcard is unique in that it identifies the natural landmarks (top) shown in the panoramic photograph (bottom), including Tenaya Canyon, Half Dome, and multiple peaks on the crest of the High Sierra.

Arthur C. Pillsbury produced this real-photo postcard with a stunning view of Half Dome, Vernal Fall, and Nevada Fall. He built up a large and successful Yosemite photography business beginning in 1906 and sold a substantial number of scenic postcards. Pillsbury provided Yosemite postcards until 1924, when the concessionaire started to produce its own.

The Glacier Point Geology Hut or Lookout, also known as an outpost of the Yosemite Museum, was constructed in 1925. The postcard is printed with "Glacier Point, above the Valley Rim, commands a magnificent view of the High Sierra. Spread before the eye is one of the world's grandest panoramas of domes and waterfalls dominated by Half Dome, which rises almost 5,000 feet above the Valley Floor."

On August 9, 1969, an electrical fire started on the bottom floor of the unoccupied Glacier Point Hotel, which, together with Mountain House, completely burned down within an hour. The hotels were never rebuilt, and a granite amphitheater now occupies the site. There is still some evidence of the old foundation of the Glacier Point Hotel. This is one of the last Glacier Point postcards published before the fire.

Seven

THE HIGH SIERRA CAMPS

In 1916, the park's concessionaire began building accommodations in Yosemite's high country to relieve congestion in Yosemite Valley and encourage people to explore the magnificent backcountry. Tuolumne Meadows High Sierra Camp was one of the first canvas tent camps built that year. The camps were forced to close in 1918 because of World War I and changes of the concessionaire, only to be reopened and expanded in 1923.

By the 1930s, the Tuolumne Meadows High Sierra Camp was the most popular of several seasonal camps, mostly because of its location along the Tioga Road. The 1935 construction of this mess hall and kitchen led to the camp becoming Tuolumne Meadows Lodge. The rustic structure built by the California Conservation Corps still serves as a lounge, dining room, and kitchen to accommodate the guests of more than 60 tents.

This 1940s postcard is of the back of the Tuolumne Meadows Lodge building, an area used for nightly campfires. The lodge is located in a conifer forest at the end of an access road, about 1.5 miles from the Tioga Road. This lodge and the other High Sierra camps are only open during the summer season but provide a great way to experience Yosemite's high country.

The Tioga Pass Road was important for accessing Yosemite from the east. The first part of the road, from Crane Flat to Tioga Pass, was completed by 1883, but the second part of the construction was more challenging. It was not until 1910 that this monumental engineering task was finished, providing a narrow road through Lee Vining Canyon along a steep drop-off to Lee Vining Creek. (Courtesy of Jerry Kell.)

In 1934, the California Conservation Corps completed this new concrete two-span road bridge across the Tuolumne River at Tuolumne Meadows. This postcard was mailed on July 12, 1953, and the back says, "As far as I remember this is the nicest camp we have ever been, although very primitive. Yesterday we climbed Mount Hoffman, what an unforgettable view from way up there. We climbed over several snowfields."

Tuolumne Meadows is the largest subalpine meadow in the Sierra Nevada and sits at an elevation of 8,600 feet on the eastern side of Yosemite National Park. The Tuolumne River winds through the meadow surrounded by majestic peaks and domes. This postcard is of the Tuolumne River passing under a footbridge and provides a splendid view of Mammoth Peak along the ridge of Kuna Crest.

Parsons Memorial Lodge, built as the Sierra Club's headquarters in 1915, was one of the earliest stone rustic buildings in a national park. Named after Edward Taylor Parsons, who served as the club's director during its fight against flooding the Hetch Hetchy Valley, the lodge is architecturally significant for its use of natural materials in an area with harsh environmental conditions. The National Park Service acquired the building in 1973.

This 1930s Soda Springs postcard shows a structure built around 1889. The small cabin was built directly over a natural spring to prevent the grazing stock from polluting the spring. This cabin is all that remains of the pioneer homestead of John Baptiste Lembert, the first settler of European descent in the Tuolumne Meadows region. He made a significant contribution as a naturalist by collecting Yosemite specimens.

A walk-in campground located near Parsons Lodge and the Soda Springs cabin was operated as a private campground for Sierra Club members. In 1972, the club signed the land over to the National Park Service, which operated the campground for the public until 1976. The fire pits and the benches were then removed, and the land has returned back to its natural setting.

This postcard showcases the "catch of the day" for a group of Tuolumne Meadow campers. The fish are likely brown or brook trout, and on the left are a couple of Sierra Nevada yellow-legged frogs. Originally, trout were only found in the valley, but in the late 1800s, Arthur G. Fletcher from the California Fish and Game Commission directed the stocking of fish in the lakes and streams of Tuolumne Meadows. (Courtesy of the California State Library.)

The alpine lakes have always been hiking attractions for visitors to the high country. Elizabeth Lake is one of the closest to Tuolumne Meadows Lodge, at just three miles away. This 1940s postcard shows the imposing backdrop of Unicorn Peak on this glacial lake. In 1909, Robert Marshall of the US Geological Survey named this lake after his niece Elizabeth Simmons.

This humorous 1940s postcard shows a black bear deciding which Tuolumne Meadows trail to follow. The bear activity has always been higher in the high country of Yosemite National Park than in the valley, especially along the Lyell Fork of the Tuolumne River in Lyell Canyon.

Easy access from the Tioga Road makes Tenaya Lake one of the most popular lakes in Tuolumne Meadows. The lake was named after Chief Tenaya by the Mariposa Battalion, who met him near its shores in the 1850s. The chief insisted that the lake was already named "Lake of the Shining Rocks." In 1868, John Muir wrote about the lake's beauty and timelessness in *My First Summer in the Sierra.*

Glen Aulin High Sierra Camp was established in 1927 as one of seven high country camps providing lodging for people who wished to experience the backcountry without carrying their own supplies. Glen Aulin, which means "beautiful valley" in Gaelic, is located next to the Tuolumne River at an elevation of 7,800 feet. The camp consists of a series of tent cabins, including this stone cookhouse built in 1935.

Waterwheel Falls, one of the largest of the Tuolumne River waterfalls, has always been a popular day-trip destination for Glen Aulin campers. This unusual "backward water wheel" falls drives an upward movement of the water caused by flow deflections from several ledges. The falls are most impressive when the high water of early summer combines with strong winds that lift the spray and blow it back upward, like a waterwheel.

The trail to Glen Aulin Camp from Tuolumne Lodge is 7.6 miles long and is considered one of the easiest trails to a High Sierra Camp. The trail follows the Tuolumne River most of the way to the encampment, which is located beside the White Cascade waterfall and its adjoining pool. The camp provides a great base for exploring the fascinating Grand Canyon of the Tuolumne.

This 1930 postcard is of Booth Lake as well as one of the five original High Sierra camps established on the north shore of the lake in 1924. Booth Lake is the largest of a group of lakes located between Fletcher and Emeric Creeks, southwest of the Tuolumne Pass. Poor drainage and an abundance of mosquitoes led to the camp's relocation to Vogelsang in the early 1930s.

Vogelsang High Sierra Camp is the highest camp, located at an elevation of 10,300 feet at the base of Fletcher Peak near Fletcher Lake. The camp had two previous sites before moving to this location in 1940, and the alpine setting makes it a favorite. The camp's name is derived from the nearby Vogelsang Pass and Peak and commemorates Charles Vogelsang, a former president of the California State Board of Fish and Game.

A popular day hike, or mule ride in this case, from Vogelsang High Sierra Camp up to Vogelsang Pass rewards one with the grandest views in Yosemite National Park. This postcard provides a southeast view toward the Cathedral and Clark Ranges at more than 10,000 feet in elevation.

The trail from Vogelsang to Merced
Lake travels downhill along Fletcher
Creek and leads to incredibly stunning
meadows. The High Sierra Camps were
established to be an easy day's walk apart,
although horses and mules have always
been available. The creek, lake, meadow,
and peak in this part of Tuolumne were
named after Arthur G. Fletcher, who
was instrumental in stocking trout in
Yosemite's alpine lakes in the late 1800s.

Merced Lake Camp has the largest
capacity of the High Sierra camps yet it is
the furthest from any trailhead. This first
camp, built by the Desmond Company
in 1916, had an office, lounge, dining
room, and kitchen. In 1922, it became
a boys' camp, complete with tennis and
basketball courts and a baseball field.
Situated along one of the largest lakes in
Yosemite, it once included rowboats.

Sunrise Camp, accessible from several trails, was named for its spectacular morning views. The nine cabins and dining tent were dedicated on July 15, 1961, as the last of the camps, completing the 50-mile High Sierra Camp Loop. Mary Curry Tresidder, who ran the private concessionaire in the park with her husband, was the camp's biggest supporter, as she believed people should have better access to the high country.

White Wolf Camp and Lodge are approximately one mile from Tioga Road. The area was developed as early as the late 1800s for supplying the silver mines; although, it is presumed to have been used as a Native America camp before that time. In 1927, John Meyer turned it into a resort with tents, cabins, a store, and a restaurant. The National Park Service bought the land and structures in the 1950s.

Eight

SENTINEL HOTEL
AND THE VILLAGES

In 1876, George Coulter and A.J. Murphy built the Sentinel Hotel, first called the Yosemite Falls Hotel, on the banks of the Merced River near Sentinel Bridge. The hotel was considered the valley's most popular lodging facility until the early 1900s, providing spectacular views of Half Dome and Yosemite Falls. The hotel was located across from Cedar Cottage, the former Hutchings House and Upper Hotel.

Oak Cottage (first right) was one of several buildings constructed by James Hutchings during the 1870s across from the Sentinel Hotel. Next to Oak Cottage is Cedar Cottage (second right), formerly known as Hutchings House, the oldest building in the complex. In 1863, pioneer entrepreneur James Hutchings bought and renovated the Upper Hotel and operated it as Hutchings House; it was renamed Cedar Cottage in 1870.

In 1866, James Hutchings added a kitchen, which also served as a sitting room, to the Hutchings House. Not willing to cut down a 175-foot incense cedar, he built around it. Eight feet in diameter, the base of the live tree became the centerpiece of the "Big Tree Room." Hutchings House became known as Cedar Cottage, and the Big Tree Room became a parlor of the Sentinel Hotel.

This 1919 postcard shows the Sentinel Hotel on the right, River Cottage on the left, and Yosemite Falls in the background. The Sentinel Hotel complex had six units by 1900. The back reads, "This is a grand place, walked up to Sentinel Dome this morning, great view and a nice climb. There are big crowds here. I certainly have enjoyed the cooking. They send mail twice a day from here."

In the early 1900s, the Sentinel Hotel monopolized accommodations in the valley. It was the only hotel there for some period of time and was centrally located for trips to the various tourist sites. As the first stop for stages entering the valley, it became an important place for mail and delivery. Additional buildings were added to support these services, eventually forming the Old Yosemite Village.

The Sentinel Hotel found most of its success in the summer season. The hotel was seldom open in the winter because it had not been weatherized when it was built in the 1870s and it occupied a particularly cold part of the valley.

Providing winter accommodations in Yosemite became increasingly important for the concessionaire in the 1920s. At that time, discussion was taking place to relocate the village, which meant tearing down the old village buildings that had developed south of the hotel complex. The Sentinel Hotel, River Cottage, and Ivy Cottages were torn down in 1938. Cedar Cottage, the oldest building in the group, was the last to be demolished in 1941.

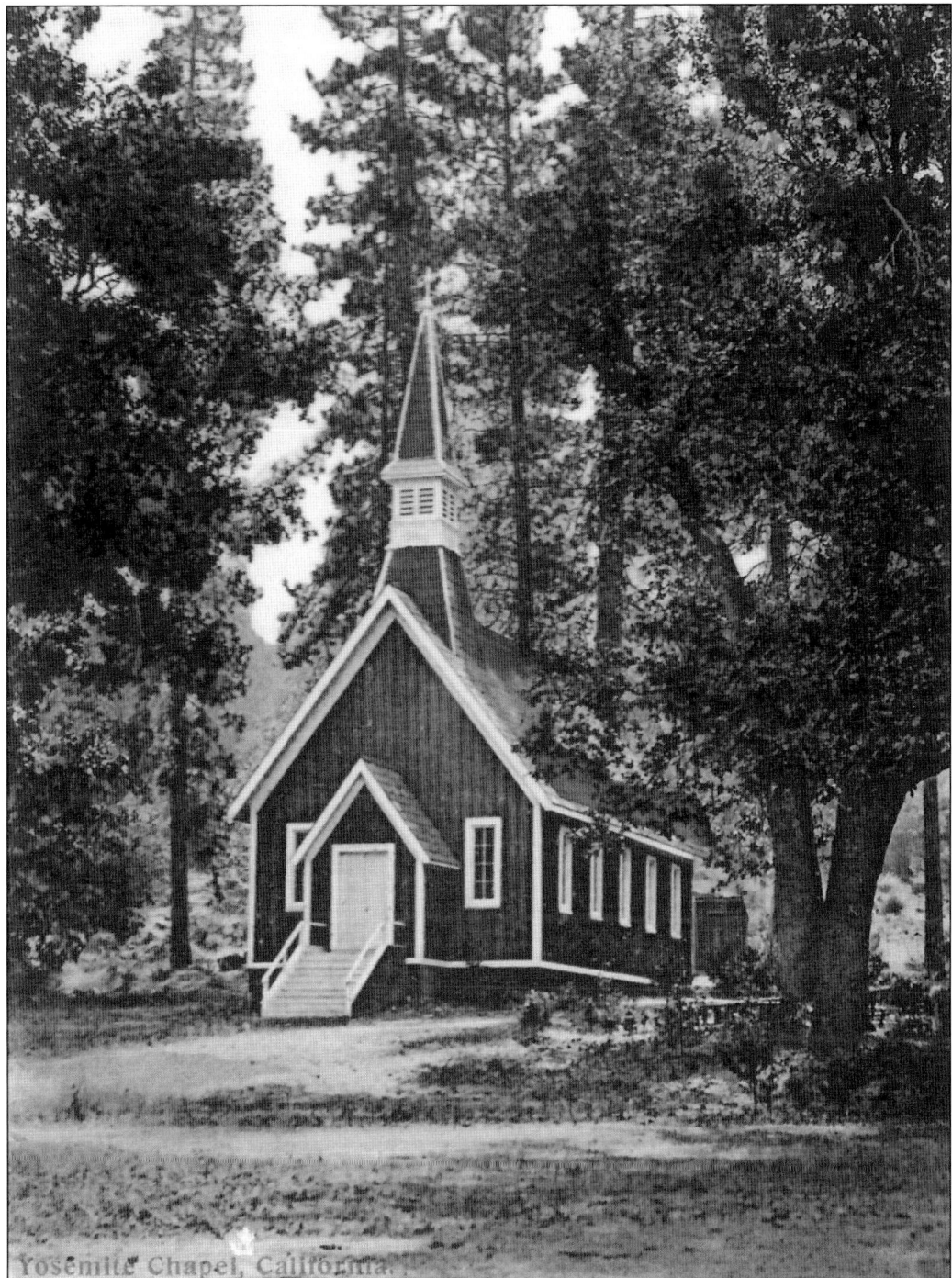

Yosemite Chapel, California.

The Yosemite Chapel is the oldest existing public structure in the park. It was built in 1879 with funds raised by the California State Sunday School Association. The original location of the structure was near the base of the Four-Mile Trail leading to Glacier Point from the lower village. In 1901, the chapel was moved about a mile to its current site, after the surrounding lower village had disappeared.

Charles Geddes, a talented architect from San Francisco, designed the New England–style Yosemite Chapel. The building, with its steep roof and prominent steeple, was restored in the 1960s and retains much of its structural integrity. The building came into National Park Service ownership in 1927. In 1973, the Yosemite Chapel became the first Yosemite structure listed in the National Register of Historic Places.

The chapel originally consisted of only one room, but an addition was added to the back of the church. The chapel's interior layout consists of a center aisle with nine rows of pews on each side, allowing seating for approximately 125 people. The chapel remains the sole church facility in the park. As stipulated in its original charter, it serves all faiths and is open all year.

Several groups of Native Americans occupied Yosemite Valley thousands of years before the European Americans arrived. They were hunters and gatherers and lived in both seasonal and permanent camps. This postcard, mailed in 1912, pictures an O'Chum, a dwelling made of small poles covered with cedar bark.

O'Chum, an Indian Tepee, Yosemite, Cal.

In the early 1900s, Yosemite's native people were living in dwellings such as the one illustrated by this postcard. By the early 1930s, the National Park Service felt the need to provide alternative housing options for the Yosemite natives who were still living in the park. Fifteen three-room cabins were constructed west of Camp 4; they were removed in 1969.

Indian Village, Yosemite Valley, Cal.

Yosemite's Native American women worked primarily around their camps, including gathering nuts, plants, and berries. The men went hunting and fishing. There was no need to farm or raise domestic animals because of the abundance of vegetation and wildlife. The Yosemite tribes also traded goods, including acorn meal and woven baskets, with other groups outside the valley.

Mary. of the Yosemite Band. Yosemite Valley, Cal.

There are several vintage postcards of Yosemite natives, including this one of a woman known as Mary and sometimes referred to as Indian Mary or China Mary. These natives of Yosemite, mostly known to come from a group called the Miwoks, became an important tourist attraction.

Chris Brown, who performed under the name Chief Lemee, was a popular and skilled dancer and storyteller at the Yosemite Museum from 1930 to 1950. He was born in 1903 of Miwok and Paiute ancestry and learned many of the ceremonial dances and chants associated with the Miwok tribal rituals. Traditional clothing was an important part of his demonstrations, and this postcard shows him in Lakita Sioux regalia.

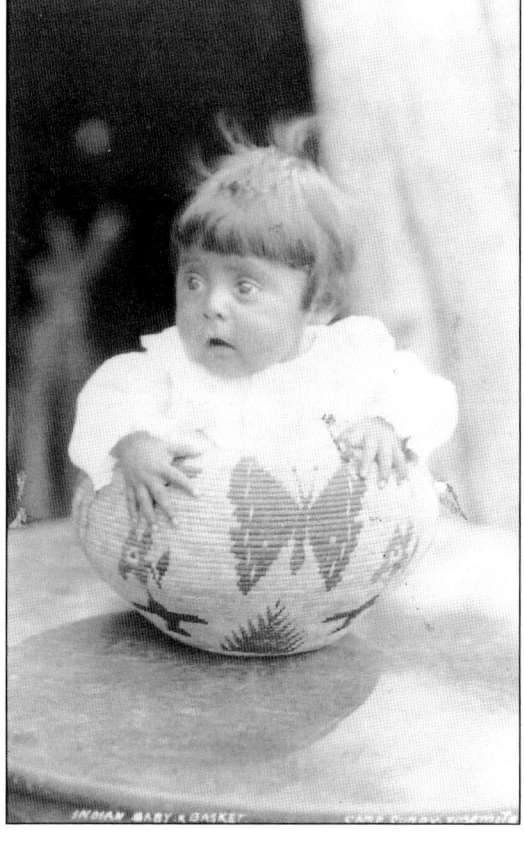

Yosemite's native peoples are famous for their basket weaving. This is a famous photograph postcard that was postmarked in 1954 from the Yosemite Lodge post office. The baby, Norman James, is sitting inside a coiled basket. His mother was Alice James Wilson, the sister of famous basket weaver Lucy Telles.

The area near the Sentinel Hotel included a post office, a store, a variety of shops, and several photograph studios. The increasing congestion on this main road and the occasional flooding of the river made the old village a less-than-ideal location for a commercial center. In the 1930s, plans were made to remove these wood-frame buildings, and Yosemite Village was built to the north.

The A-frame building in Yosemite Village was constructed in the 1950s and houses Degnan's Deli. John and Bridget Degnan settled in Yosemite in 1884, and by 1900, Bridget's baking skills had developed into Degnan's Bakery and Kitchen, which was a successful family business for more than 50 years. The bakery's previous location was in the old village next to the chapel. This pioneer business was sold to Yosemite's concessionaire in 1974.

The Sierra Club constructed LeConte Memorial Lodge in 1904. The building was named for Joseph LeConte, a renowned professor of geology who died at Camp Curry on July 5, 1901. This 1908 postcard reflects the lodge's original location at the base of Glacier Point next to Camp Curry. In order to accommodate Camp Curry's expansion, it moved west across from Housekeeping Camp and reopened in 1919.

The Tudor-style architecture of the LeConte Memorial Lodge is extremely unusual for a national park. The building, whose prevailing architectural feature is its steep roof, has three rooms—a central meeting room flanked by two smaller rooms. It was Yosemite's first visitors' center. Today, it is owned by the National Park Service and the Sierra Club and continues to be used for various educational purposes.

Nine

THE AHWAHNEE

The Ahwahnee Hotel, completed in 1927 and located approximately one mile east of Yosemite Village, is Yosemite's luxury hotel and an architectural masterpiece. Stephen Mather, the first director of the National Park Service, was influential in gathering support and funding for this year-round hotel. The enormous hotel structure was designed by Los Angeles architect Gilbert Stanley Underwood and has six floors including a penthouse.

The Miwoks, a Yosemite Native American group, were the original occupants of this meadow surrounded by oak trees near the banks of the Merced River. In the 1880s, it became Kennyville, a stable complex that serviced horse and stage transportation until the 1920s. The splendid views of Half Dome, Glacier Point, Royal Arches, and Yosemite Falls were important factors leading to the selection of this location for a first-class hotel.

This postcard, as seen from the south lawn, is of one of the three wings of the hotel. The south side is considered the back of the hotel, but the original plan was for it to be the front. Due to poor ventilation design, the front entrance was changed—just 10 days before the grand opening—from where the Ahwahnee Bar is to the location with the covered walkway today.

SKIING AT THE AHWAHNEE • YOSEMITE

The completion of a hotel that was open year-round led to increasing interest in winter sports. This 1930s vintage postcard is part of a series of postcards used to promote winter activities in Yosemite. These cross-country skiers are on the south side of the Ahwahnee Hotel grounds, where they have a stunning view of Yosemite Falls.

ELEVATOR LOBBY - THE AHWANEE

The Elevator Lobby is at the center of the hotel, in a space beyond the Main Lobby leading to either the dining room or the Great Lounge. Guests use this as a waiting area for the dining room or to lounge by the fire. The large fireplace is faced with native jasper, as is the staircase (not pictured), which leads to the mezzanine and formerly the women's lounge.

The Ahwahnee - Lounge Room - Yosemite

The original painted mural above the fireplace in the Elevator Lobby depicts swirling and overlapping Native American baskets and was created by artist Jeannette Dyer Spencer, who was hired as resident artist of the Ahwahnee Hotel in 1926. The patterns from Native American baskets and rugs can be seen throughout the hotel. Large open entrances on both sides of the fireplace lead into the Great Lounge.

The Great Lounge is a large room with 24-foot ceilings and 10 floor-to-ceiling windows that provide a sense of grandeur. Interior designers Arthur Upham Pope and Phyllis Ackerman are credited for adding splendor to the Great Lounge by combining Native American, Middle Eastern, and Art Deco styles.

This postcard of the Great Lounge from the 1940s provides a glimpse of the ceiling's exposed beams. These beams were painted, each with a different border design, by artist Jeannette Dyer Spencer. The wrought-iron chandeliers hanging throughout the hotel have a German Gothic design combined with Native American detailing.

THE AHWAHNEE LOUNGE ROOM

Fire Place in The Ahwahnee Lounge Room

Two enormous fireplaces flank the Great Lounge. This 1940s postcard shows the fireplace at the south end of the room with Native American baskets displayed across the mantel. At the time, Persian rugs covered the hardwood floors and also adorned the walls. These vintage postcards of the Ahwahnee Hotel's interior uniquely capture the decorations of the room during that period.

The two enormous fireplaces in the lounge were designed with sandstone and include built-in benches. The hearths are tall enough to stand under and were scaled to counter the magnitude of the grand room. One of the many Persian rugs displayed throughout the hotel hangs above the fireplace. The original interior designers, Arthur Upham Pope and Phyllis Ackerman, who were experts in Persian arts, integrated the rugs.

In 1943, the Navy converted the Ahwahnee Hotel into a convalescent hospital to rehabilitate Navy personnel serving in World War II. The Great Lounge was transformed into a ward with four rows of bunk beds. The building was renovated to become a hotel again in 1946 and opened for guests in December. One of the dramatic changes made during the Great Lounge's renovations was this new design for the mural.

Fran Spencer Reynolds, the daughter of artist Jeannette Dyer Spencer, designed the new mural for the Great Lounge. She was appointed to create a mural of Mondrian style above the fireplace on the Great Lounge's north wall. The mural remained until the early 1980s, when the original 1927 appearance was restored.

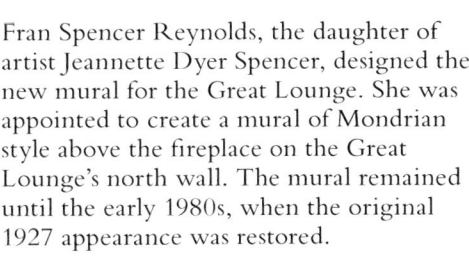

THE AHWAHNEE LOUNGE ROOM

The hotel is a massive structure with three wings, and this postcard provides a view of the south wing. The hotel has steel framework, is faced with local granite, and is sided with concrete shaped and stained to look like redwood boards and beams. This fireproof structure that blends with the natural environment is truly a masterpiece.

The stone columns surrounding the hotel's exterior are made of local granite and blend with the natural surroundings. The architect insisted the worn and battered surface of the granite be visible and that larger stones be placed at the bottom of the pillars for a more natural look. These well-planned and executed exterior design features make the Ahwahnee Hotel one of the world's finest hotels in a natural setting.

THE AHWAHNEE SOLARIUM

The Solarium is located in the south wing of the hotel and overlooks an expansive meadow. The semicircular room is surrounded by five floor-to-ceiling windows, which provide a sunny atmosphere and a magnificent view of Glacier Point. The Solarium is the perfect setting for wedding receptions and special events, which have taken place there since the hotel opened in 1927.

Almost every room in the hotel has a fireplace, with the exception of the Solarium. The focal feature in this room is a fountain made of local jasper rock from a Mariposa County quarry. Ferns and other plants surround the trickling water fountain. Above the fountain is the landing of the stairway that leads to the Tudor Lounge, which overlooks the Great Lounge.

THE AHWAHNEE SOLARIUM

The Ahwahnee dining room is considered to be one of the most beautiful and stunning dining facilities in a national park. Every detail of this large room was designed to provide an elegant dining experience while filling the room with the splendor of its natural surroundings. This postcard looks toward the main entrance and provides a good view of the large pine framework used to support the ceiling.

The dining room seats almost 350 people and is supported by a kitchen originally intended for a much larger hotel. The enormous kitchen with its own pastry and bake stations had already been designed when plans for the hotel were downsized, but the kitchen's size was not reduced. This postcard shows the massive granite indoor pillars of the dining room and the use of Native American designs in the decor.

This 1950s postcard looking into the massive dining room provides a good view of the granite pillars, which are interspersed with floor-to-ceiling windows. The manufacturing and transport of the large window glass was quite an accomplishment in the 1920s. The southern exposure of the dining room provides for magnificent lighting and incredible views of Yosemite's natural landmarks.

This postcard provides a nice view of the "tree trunks" that support the trusses. These logs are actually concrete that has been molded and stained to look like wood. The dining room has retained its original wooden furniture and unique wrought-iron chandeliers. This dining room serves breakfast, lunch, and dinner.

The California Room extends out from the Great Lounge and was originally decorated with items from the Gold Rush days, including the polar bear rugs seen in this postcard. When the California Room became the headquarters of the Yosemite Winter Club, the room was refurnished, and the walls of the room were decorated with photographs and artifacts of winter activities.

El Dorado Diggins on the mezzanine level was originally a private dining room but, after the Prohibition era, it was transformed into a Gold Rush–themed bar, complete with a false storefront and antiques. The room was also changed into a chapel when the Navy used the hotel for convalescing servicemen in the 1940s. Today, this room is one of the hotel's most luxurious suites and includes the park's only Jacuzzi.

Ten

THE LODGE AND
BADGER PASS

Yosemite Falls is one of the tallest waterfalls in North America and a spectacular attraction for visitors to Yosemite National Park. Yosemite Lodge's proximity to the falls and its more moderate pricing for hotel rooms compared to the Ahwahnee Hotel has always made this a popular accommodation. This 1920s postcard of Yosemite Lodge's covered entrance illustrates its vicinity to Yosemite Falls.

The Yosemite Lodge site was initially developed by the US Army, whose park headquarters was relocated here from Wawona in 1906. The soldiers at Fort Yosemite were responsible for administering and protecting the park until 1916, when the National Park Service was established and took control. This postcard shows the main building of the old Army camp after it was remodeled into a tourist lodge.

The Desmond Park Service Company was the concessionaire that began leasing the former Army campsite and renovating the Army barracks in 1916. The company also bought prefabricated cabins, which were transported by train to El Portal and trucked into Yosemite Valley for assembly. These popular cabins provided both privacy and charm and were used until 1999.

With Yosemite Lodge's opening to the public in 1916 came an important contribution to winter accommodations in Yosemite Valley. Before 1927, the Sentinel Hotel was the only other lodging open during the winter and it was often found to be less than ideal in the weather conditions seen in this postcard.

This 1940s postcard shows the proximity of the Yosemite Lodge cabins to the Merced River. Many of these cabins were destroyed during one of Yosemite's worst floods in January 1997, when a total of 189 cabins and 108 hotel rooms at Yosemite Lodge were damaged or destroyed by the flooding of the Merced River. These cabins are no longer available as accommodations at the Yosemite Lodge.

Pine Cottage, designed to reflect early California architecture, was built in 1950 along Yosemite Creek. As part of the Yosemite Lodge complex, it added 32 units, half of those with baths. During the 1997 flood, Pine Cottage was submerged in eight feet of water and had to be torn down. The site has not been redeveloped and therefore returned to its natural state. (Courtesy of the California State Library.)

When the Desmond Park Service Company remodeled and converted the Army barracks beginning in 1916, it added a cafeteria and grill south of Yosemite Lodge's main building.

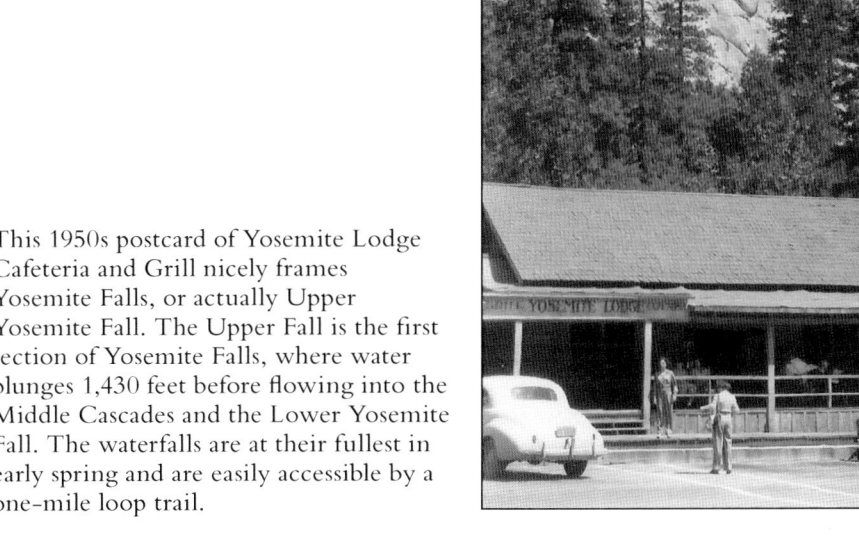

This 1950s postcard of Yosemite Lodge Cafeteria and Grill nicely frames Yosemite Falls, or actually Upper Yosemite Fall. The Upper Fall is the first section of Yosemite Falls, where water plunges 1,430 feet before flowing into the Middle Cascades and the Lower Yosemite Fall. The waterfalls are at their fullest in early spring and are easily accessible by a one-mile loop trail.

In 1956, the National Park Service sponsored the Mission 66 program, which would span a 10-year period with the goal of increasing park visitation and expanding services. For Yosemite Lodge, this meant a new complex, which was composed essentially of four redwood buildings connected to each other by covered walkways.

The popular Mountain Room Lounge with its large windows and open-air fireplace was a favorite meeting place for guests after a day of hiking or sightseeing. The decorative plates around the fireplace came from the hearth at Badger Pass Ski Area, as that lodge resort was also remodeled in the 1950s. The Mountain Room Lounge was added to the Yosemite Lodge during the 1950s renovations and includes an outside seating area.

SKIING IN YOSEMITE NATIONAL PARK

The completion of the Ahwahnee Hotel in 1927 led to increasing interest in developing winter activities to make Yosemite a year-round destination. The Yosemite Ski School was established in 1928 and is considered one of the first ski schools in California. It immediately brought in experienced European ski instructors to provide elaborate ski excursions to Yosemite's high country. Yosemite even put in a bid for the 1932 Winter Olympics.

SKIING IN YOSEMITE NATIONAL PARK

Efforts to expand winter sports out of the valley included the introduction of ski touring. A series of winter huts in the park allowed cross-country skiers to travel from one hut to another, just as they can in the European Alps. In 1930, the Snow Creek Ski Cabin was constructed on the slope of Mount Watkins, and two Tuolumne Meadows cabins were converted into ski huts.

121

This 1940s postcard shows Chinquapin store and gas station, which is located midway between Wawona and Yosemite Valley on Highway 140 at Glacier Point Road. Chinquapin was developed as a downhill ski area in 1932–1933, and the service station was used as a day lodge for skiers. For a couple of winters, Chinquapin was the principal place in Yosemite National Park for downhill skiing.

The popularity of downhill skiing in the 1930s drove Yosemite's concessionaires to search for more elaborate and challenging ski slopes. A site was identified approximately six miles up the Glacier Point Road and above Monroe Meadow for Badger Pass Ski Area, which was established in 1934. The need for a ski house led to the completion and dedication of the Badger Pass Ski Lodge in December 1935. (Courtesy of Jerry Kell.)

The Badger Pass Ski Lodge was designed in park service rustic style, a type of architecture that incorporates the natural setting surrounding a structure. The two-story log building, with elements of the Swiss Chalet style, served as a ski house and lounge without overnight accommodations for visitors. It was one of the first downhill ski lodges in California and the first one located in a Western national park.

This postcard from the late 1930s overlooks one of the primary ski slopes near the Badger Pass Ski Lodge. The runs were widened and the trails cleared in the years following the area's opening. The building in this postcard is the motor room for the Up-Ski or sled, better known as the Queen Mary, named after Mary Curry Tressider. In 1946, the Up-Ski was replaced by a T-bar ski lift. (Courtesy of Jerry Kell.)

BADGER PASS SKI LODGE FIRE PLACE

The Badger Pass Ski Lodge provided storage for ski equipment and the opportunity to lounge on the deck or near this fireplace. The large fireplace in the lounge was decorated with cast-iron metal panels from artist Robert Boardman Howard. The fireplace was removed during the 1950s renovations, but some of the decorative panels were saved and built into the fireplace in the Mountain Room Lounge at Yosemite Lodge.

This 1948 postcard shows snowplows clearing the Badger Pass road and parking lot. As early as 1938, the shortage of parking at the Badger Pass Ski Lodge was a problem. The original parking capacity was 200 cars. In 1941, the parking area was increased to accommodate 400 cars and, in 1958, enlarged again to hold 665 cars. Since then, even more parking has been added. (Courtesy of Jerry Kell.)

In 1954, Badger Pass Ski Lodge was enlarged, and another building was added and connected to the lodge by a breezeway. The completion of Badger Pass Ski Area in 1934 made it one of the first developed ski areas in California and really marked the beginning of skiing as a popular recreational activity. Badger Pass Ski Area is one of two existing ski areas located within a national park.

The printing on the back of this 1960s postcard says, "Snowmobiles make scheduled tours of the ski area at Badger Pass." This image captures a snow tour on a Bombardier Snow Cat just as it passes Old Badger Pass Summit. The Snow Cat tours were discontinued in the early 1990s.

The Badger Pass Ski Area served as the venue for professional and downhill ski competitions from the 1930s through the 1950s, including California's first National Ski Championships. In the 1950s, the park service decided to discontinue the support of spectator sports in order to maintain the area's natural beauty. The ski resort then transitioned to a more family-focused environment that catered to skiers of all skill levels.

BIBLIOGRAPHY

Greene, Linda. *Yosemite: The Park and Its Resources: A History of the Discovery, Management and Physical Development of Yosemite National Park, California.* Yosemite, CA: National Park Service, 1987.

Johnston, Hank. *Railroads of the Yosemite Valley.* Glendale, CA: Trans-Anglo Books, 1995.

———. *Yosemite's Yesterdays.* Palm Springs, CA: Flying Spur Press, 1989.

Sargent, Shirley. *The Ahwahnee: Yosemite's Classic Hotel.* Yosemite, CA: Yosemite Park & Curry Company, 1977.

———. *Yosemite's High Sierra Camps.* Yosemite, CA: Flying Spurr Press, 1977.

———. *Yosemite's Historic Wawona.* Yosemite, CA: Flying Spur Press, 1984.

———. *Yosemite's Innkeepers: The story of a great park and its chief concessionaires.* Yosemite, CA: Ponderosa Press, 2000.

Radanovich, Leroy. *Yosemite Valley: Images of America*, Charleston, SC: Arcadia Publishing.

Russell, Carl P. *One Hundred Years in Yosemite: The story of a great park and its friends.* Yosemite National Park, CA: Yosemite National History Association, 1968.

Walklet, Keith. *The Ahwahnee: Yosemite's Grand Hotel.* Yosemite, CA: DNC Parks and Resorts at Yosemite, Inc., 2004.

Discover Thousands of Local History Books
Featuring Millions of Vintage Images

Arcadia Publishing, the leading local history publisher in the United States, is committed to making history accessible and meaningful through publishing books that celebrate and preserve the heritage of America's people and places.

Find more books like this at
www.arcadiapublishing.com

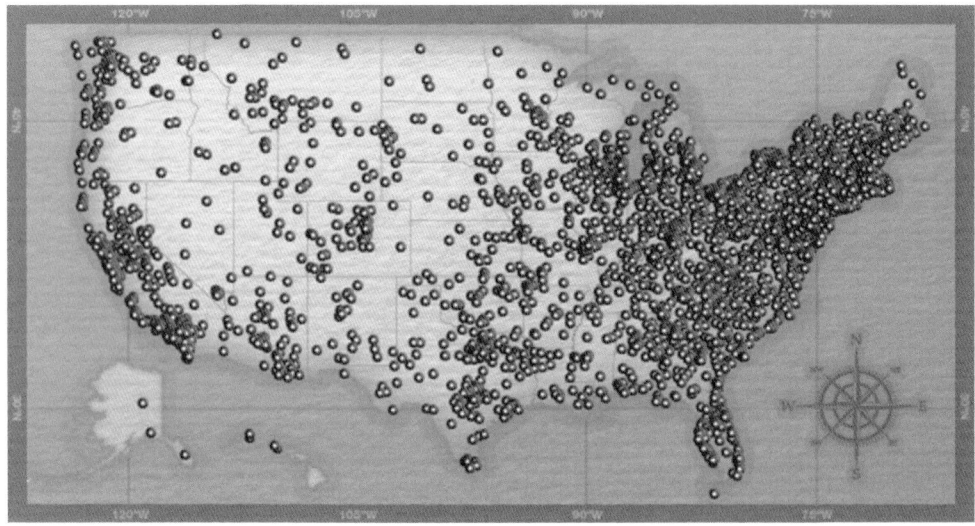

Search for your hometown history, your old stomping grounds, and even your favorite sports team.

Consistent with our mission to preserve history on a local level, this book was printed in South Carolina on American-made paper and manufactured entirely in the United States. Products carrying the accredited Forest Stewardship Council (FSC) label are printed on 100 percent FSC-certified paper.

MADE IN THE
USA